For our dear niece Dara,
with all our love and admiration in
every magical adventure you undertake.

to all the little girls in the world,
may you discover the magic and
strength you carry within you every day.

the Princess and the Rainbow Unicorn

DAIAN BOOKS

In the kingdom of Fantasia, Princess Dara woke up with a strange feeling.

Looking out his tower window, she realized something wasn't quite right.

the colors of the sky, normally bright and vibrant, seemed to be slowly fading.

Worried, Dara called her faithful friend, Flash, a magical unicorn.

With his snow-white fur and a glowing horn on his forehead, Flash was always ready to help the brave princess on any adventure.

together, they decided to
investigate what was happening to
the kingdom's colors.

With determination, Dara and Flash prepared to face whatever awaited them within the fortress and put an end to the mystery behind the lost colors of their kingdom.

While exploring the kingdom,
Dara and Flash noticed that even
the brightest flowers and lushest
trees were losing their color.

the princess realized that something
terrible was happening,
and knew that they had to find a
way to stop it.

With bravery in their hearts, Dara and Flash prepared to embark on an exciting adventure to discover the cause of the colors' disappearance and save their beloved kingdom of Fantasia.

the path to the answer was full of mysteries and dangers.

Dara and Flash entered the dark forests and crossed the silent fields, searching for clues that could lead them to the truth behind the colors disappearing.

On their journey, they
encountered forest creatures
who were also concerned about
the loss of colors.

Elves, fairies, and magical animals shared stories about how their homes were losing their sparkle and charm.

Finally, they reached the edge of the kingdom, where a dark and sinister fortress stood.

Dara felt a chill run down her spine as she looked at the place, but she knew they had to keep going if they wanted to discover the truth.

With a firm step, Dara and Flash entered the fortress, prepared to confront the mysterious sorcerer responsible for the disappearance of the colors.

the interior was dark and silent, full of shadows that seemed to lurk around every corner.

Suddenly, a sinister voice rang through the air, announcing the arrival of the sorcerer.

From the shadows emerged a hooded figure, with glowing eyes filled with malice and a dark aura enveloping his being.

the sorcerer taunted Dara and Flash, revealing that he had stolen the kingdom's colors to fuel his dark magic and dominate Fantasia.

But the princess and her faithful unicorn were not afraid; they were determined to stop him and restore joy and color to their home.

An epic battle erupted in the fortress, with rays of light and shadows colliding in a frantic dance.

Dara and Flash fought bravely, using their friendship and determination to confront the sorcerer and his dark magic.

Can Dara and Flash defeat the sorcerer and restore colors to the kingdom of Fantasy?

the exciting conclusion is
yet to come!

the battle reached its climax when Dara and Flash faced the sorcerer with all their strength and determination.

With each swing of the
sword and burst of light,
they came closer to the
victory they so longed for.

With one last effort, Dara channeled all his courage and power, casting a spell that sent the sorcerer to a dark and distant dimension, far from the realm of Fantasia.

With the sorcerer defeated, colors began to return to the world, bright and resplendent as never before.

With peace restored in Fantasia, Dara and Flash were hailed as heroes throughout the kingdom.

Celebrations full of joy and color spread to every corner, while grateful inhabitants honored the brave princess and her faithful unicorn.

Since then, Dara and Flash continued to protect the kingdom of Fantasia, facing challenges together and always remembering the power of friendship and courage.

And although dangers might lurk on the horizon, they knew that as long as they were together, nothing could dim the brilliance of their spirit and the light of their friendship.

the End.